A Man's Dance

Poems

By Perry Higman

To Tony & Margrit with affection & best regards —
Perry H

High Peaks Books
Anacortes, Wa.

A MAN'S DANCE. Copyright©2013 by Perry Higman and High Peaks Books. All rights reserved. Printed and bound by Village Books, Bellingham, Washington, in the United States of America. No part of this book may be used or reproduced in any manner without permission except in the case of brief quotations in reviews or critical articles. Go to Highpeaksbooks.com for information.

Please see list of photo credits for cover, back cover and interior photos.

Library of Congress Cataloging-in-Publication Data has been applied for. ISBN 978-0-615-80405-7

A MAN'S DANCE, Author's Introduction

In spite of taking lessons in the 6th grade, I am not a good dancer. Lacking this talent I have learned to dance in other ways with the world I live in. Sometimes I lead, sometimes life does. This is my agreement with the world. In these poems I have tried to hold—now with a man's confident hand—my childhood and coming of age in Mexico; my wife, children, friends; my elders and heroes; my cancer, my travels, my deep love of art, motorsports, and American music and poets; and especially my love of open country and the mountains—climbing, backcountry skiing, the cowboy life. These dances fill me with grace, love, and profound gratitude.

I am inspired by real people and places and times. These poems are all absolutely true, nothing is made-up. (As I write this I listen to Edith Piaf singing "Les Trois Cloches." Her recorded voice—what a miracle—almost always brings me to tears). This is my "Man's Dance," and I pray that in these poems you may find an invitation to your own awesome dance with life.

                                    PH

Liberty Bell Group. North Cascades, Washington.
Photo, Denny Burmeister

Larry Deaver N. Idaho backcountry. Photo by Dave Waag, *Off-Piste Magazine.* Offpistemag.com

Deb Copenhaver on Snake, Penticton, B.C. 1949.
Photo Credit, Art Chamberlain

Dick Alt, Chet Higman, Dwight Watson, Hermann Ulrichs. Climbing reconnaissance in the North Cascades, 1936. Photo by Hermann Ulrichs

Acknowledgments:

Perhaps in another life I'll be able to properly thank some of my teachers in person. 'Though they are gone, these need to be named here:

> Laverne Whipp, 9th grade English teacher at Rincon High School, Tucson, Arizona, who taught me the power of simple poems through his love of Edgar Lee Masters' *Spoon River Anthology;*
>
> Ray Johnston, band teacher at Sealth High School, who repeatedly sneaked us into the "Blue Banjo" in Pioneer Square in Seattle to hear real Dixieland;
>
> Professor Julio Durán Cerda, and his wife Martina Chacón, at the University of Iowa, who guided me in Latin American poetry and music.

Our three grown-up children, Jesse, Shelley, and Rick, keep teaching me more and more. They just recently introduced me to 'Antony' singing Leonard Cohen's "If it be His Will." Life changer.

Thanks to my second fathers: Bardomiano Balbuena, Mexican woodcutter; and to Deb Copenhaver, 1955 and 1956 World Champion Saddle Bronc rider and true Christian. I couldn't do without them.

Nothing is more necessary (or scarier) than a dead-honest critic. Thanks, Sandra.

Nothing more needed than an editor with the patience and the eye of a sniper. Thanks, Lyn Kraatz.

And nothing is better than a designer and artist like Barb Chase—Fineartbybarb.com. Thank you, Barb.

These poems ARE, and are for, my wonderful friends,

Thank you all for coming to the party,

Perry Higman

Contents, A MAN'S DANCE

The Salmon	15
A Man's Dance	17
My Rivers	20
New Moon	23
Jicaltepec, Veracruz	25
Pineapples	27
Music	29
Turning Down Lola Beltrán	33
In School	35
Blankets	37
The Pass	39
NASCAR	42
Country Sunday	46
A Man	48
A Photograph of Zapata	51
Friends	54
Love	56
Doc	59
The Cantabrian Sea	62
For Theresa Puthoff	64
Valentine's Day	67
Midway Direct	69
For Jesse	72
Art	74
Roy Rogers and Me	77
Mt. Adams	79
Holding Sydney	82
The Vietnam Veterans Memorial	85
Lines from My Father's Song	87
Unopened Gifts	90
Hawaiian Christmas Surfer	92

Lilies on the Day of Our Holy Virgin of Guadalupe	93
Butterfly	96
Meeting in Madrid	98
View from Aneto	99
Baptism	100
The Mail	101
On the Shoulder of Highway 93	103
Homestead	104
First Rain	105
Places and Men	106
One	109
Angel	110
Pinesmoke	113
Heroes	115
USS Arizona Memorial	117
The Final Step	118
The Touch of the Earth	120
Thank you Song to a Cowboy	123
Pillows	125
Iowa	126
Sandra at Sixty	127
Kona Night	129
After a Rain	131
Death Will Come to Me	132

To my mother and father,
who gave me freedom

Others may praise what they like;
But I, from the banks of the running Missouri,
praise nothing in art or aught else,
'Til it has well inhaled the atmosphere of this
  river,
also the western prairie-scent, and exudes it all
  again.

Walt Whitman

THE SALMON

It is so clear, so pure.
Even magnified by the water,
we have trouble seeing,
because the fish and the stones
look the same.
But it is not so he may be
hidden, but a sign
we all share
the single purpose.
We can sense
the vigor
of firm muscle
swum from the sea.
He has returned.

He knew at his birth
which stones and water
were the place of his death.
He knew at his birth
the dignity
of the cycle of waters.
He knew at his birth
the last touch of sun
on his back.
He has returned.

He knew at his birth
how the last flow
of water would taste.
He knew at his birth
the longing

for the climax of life.
He has returned.

The great trees watch and know.
The bears and ravens know.
I know.
I am home.

A MAN'S DANCE (for Guy and Matt Copenhaver,
Kevin and Greg Leyva, Cheryl and Lester Simmons)

>   The construction worker
>   drove
>   a loader
>
>   roaring forward
>   roaring back
>
>   in wide arcs
>   between
>   the pile of dirt
>   and truck
>
>   -- the dance
>   too powerful
>   to interrupt
>   except to share
>
>   a moment of
>   my glance.

Scraper, *Copenhaver Construction*, Creston, Washington. Photo by Guy Copenhaver

The cropduster
slid
the yellow plane up
through a tight
bank
just above
the powerline
and dropped down
to make
another trip

the dance
too serious
to interrupt
except for a quick
wing dip.

Crop duster *Greg's Crop Care*, Wilbur
Washington. Photo by Todd Rodrigues

The truckdriver
passed me
fast
the trailer pulling
bullet true
blowing through
a snowy night

-- the dance
too much a thrill
to interrupt
I think
except to quickly reach
and blink
his lights.

Cheryl and Lester Simmons, 40 years on the road together. Photo, Sandra Higman

MY RIVERS

> " . . . muddy river, just like a long-
> lost friend, roll on Mississippi,
> you make me feel like a child again."
> 'Roll on Mississippi ' Kye
> Fleming / Dennis Morgan / Charlie Pride

I am constantly drawn back
to the rivers.

While my parents watched
I ran the smooth gravel and granite
along Denny Creek
in my bare feet.

> *The rock is still warm*
> *in the sun*
> *and the water's still*
> *flowing.*

Mornings in camp
I cut kindling
and built fires
to make breakfast,
and at night
I listened to the words
of the Methow.

> *Split cedar*
> *is still in the air*
> *and the water's still*
> *flowing.*

I swam and played
in the Nautla
with boys and girls
and black snakes
until I was sleek
with tropical water.

> *Thundershaken rains*
> *still flood down from the*
> *mountains*
> *and the water's still*
> *flowing.*

In the darkness I walked
along the banks of the Iowa
holding the summer heat
tightly between her hand
and mine.

> *Firefly lights*
> *still trace through the night*
> *and the water's still*
> *flowing.*

After a day
of rock and glacier sun
on Colchuck Peak
I bathed
in the Wenatchee's
snowy waters.

> *Cold water kisses*
> *still excite me*

*and the water's still
flowing.*

And each time
I drive over the bridge
at Vantage
I wonder
how the cold water
and the wet, warm horse
felt to Qualchan
the last time he swam the Columbia
heading east to Spokane

*and knew the water
would still be
flowing.*

NEW MOON

(for my friend Peter Campbell,
on hearing of his death)

"Andrew Wood was so young,
hard to feel my priest is gone . . . "

'Sacred Life,' Ian Astbury, *The Cult*

I woke at night
before the dawn
to a new moon
in the southeast Spokane sky—
and in its still
and silent crescent
I saw Peter's face,
his eyes and smile.

It slowly faded
in the sunrise
and left me here
to see and learn
more of Peter's daily lessons
about the old people,
their gathering places,
and of the salmon
that must return.

And when the young
born every springtime,
come to know
about the moon,
and see its life

on silvery water,
and touch its death
left in the stones

they will remember
in the dark there with us
that when the new moon's
showing
the fullness of its story
is never gone.

JICALTEPEC, VERACRUZ

In Jicaltepec
as a boy
I learned of the earth,
not of the sky.

Each day
it was my job
to clean and fill
the lanterns
—to be ready
for the night—

and then
I'd run to the river
to see the fish
or sometimes an alligator
that Teodoro had caught;
or cross the muddy street
to eat the last tortillas
my friend's mother had made
for breakfast,
before they got fed
to the dog.

On Sunday mornings
we'd all gather
on the wide stone steps
of the butcher's house
to watch him
kill a cow.

And when
we'd follow the men
to the fields
to help pull weeds
or keep
the burros and mules
out of the corn,
we'd pass the solitary, burned-
    out,
bullet-riddled church

    never needed,

    never rebuilt,

    and never forgiven.

PINEAPPLES (Jicaltepec, Veracruz)

When pineapples were cheap
because the crop wouldn't keep,
we'd buy two for a peso
in the fields around San Rafael
and take them home to share.

My friend Marcos,
with his father's machete,
in one swing
would cut off the bottom,
and with two
sever
the thick sharp-leaved stem

—it looked just like
the ancient warrior's topknot
carved in a limestone rock
at the edge of town—

and then,
with a knife far too big for the job,
he'd quickly peel
its alligator skin
to the yellow insides
so we all had a round we could eat.

The buzzards above
smelling
the blue steel blade
slicing ripe fruit
mixed their black circles

into the light
of the iron-sun day

and each one of us knew
we'd be touched
by the shadows
they left on us as we played

MUSIC

"mi vida, ¿por qué te alejas?
¿por qué me dejas?
si sabes que en este mundo
sin tu cariño no he de vivir . . .
aaaaaayyyy . . . "

(" my love, why are you leaving?
why are you going away?
if you know that in this world
I can't live without your love? . . .
aaaaaayyyy . . . ")

Cuco Sánchez

I was writing
the yearly report
for the academic
program I direct . . .
listening to a tape
of 40s and 50s
Mexican canciones
rancheras . . .

From
a song about
a lost love
came
two full measures
of a plain
soft
"aaaaaaayyyyy. . ."
in three quarter time (1,2,3 /
1,2,3)
as only a Mexican

can sing it,
with the agony
of certain death
in the momentary
ecstasy of love

—a cry
I overhear
in the world
every once in a while
from a soul
who has been
dipped
into the baptismal
waters of life.

—a cry
that sings
the celestial hum
of the earth's
groundwater
flowing through
veins of rock.

—a cry
that weeps
like a woman
with the rage
of a man.

—a cry
I always
must follow

to a river
whose dark
current tries
to pull my heart
from my body

I remembered
my mother
driving Susana home
after school,
somewhere
on the east side
of Mexico City,
to a house
I could never
find again,
because I was
drowning
in love,
and I still
cannot recall
the number
or the street.

You never forget
what it feels like
to drown.

I rolled
my ring

around my finger
feeling
the smooth gold
of my desperate love
for Sandra
when we first
married,
and I knew
I would die
if she went away.

And then
I remembered
singing
this very song
to quiet my children
and put them to sleep,
and to teach them
its world
of life-giving
breath
and blood.

TURNING DOWN LOLA BELTRAN

> " . . . de pasión mortal, moría . . . "
>
> 'Cucurrucucú Paloma,' Tomás Méndez
> / Lola Beltrán

When I was twelve
I heard the voice
of Lola Beltrán
from the jukebox
in the corner cantina,
playing loud enough
to feel
in the stones
beneath my feet.

It felt like when
I was hit and pushed down
by a boy who was stronger.

I awoke
in the powerful world
of men and women
where songs
meant
what they said.

I touched her boldness
in the adobe walls,
I saw her body

in the building afternoon
storm,

the dark reflection
of her passion
in the obsidian eyes
of men
pushing in and out
of the doors.

It was a voice
you could smell in the street.

I still have
some of her records
and I play them loud
when you are not here.

When you come home
I turn the music down,
because there is
no need.

IN SCHOOL

> ". . . Have you seen God in His splendors,
> heard the text that nature renders?
> (You'll never hear it in the family pew.) . . ."
>
> "The Call of the Wild," Robert Service

In school I learned
Columbus
made a deal
with the king and queen of Spain
to search for routes of trade
to the Indies in the East.

But now
watching a sail
fill with the glittering breath
of a rising Atlantic breeze,
now I know
the king and queen
found the one
who had to go—

he loved the sea
he loved the sea
he had to cross the sea

In school I learned
President Jefferson sent
Meriwether Lewis
to walk and map
the middle of the continent
just purchased

from the French.

But now
when I see
the Missouri
rolling muddy
like blood from the heart
of the Rockies
a thousand miles away—
now I know
Mr. Jefferson found the man
who had to go—

he loved the plains
he loved the plains
he had to cross the plains

So, now I know,
from the great plains and oceans—
and on the tops of mountain peaks

(where I can feel
my own tiny being
held between the earth
and the endless sky)

—now I know
the good fortune
of men who have to go
to a place
where their daemons can dance
with beauty.

BLANKETS

> "Por caja quiero un sarape,
> por cruz mis dobles cananas,
> y escriban sobre mi tumba,
> mi último adiós con mil balas,
> ay, ay, corazón ¿por qué no amas?"
>
> 'La cama de piedra,' Cuco Sánchez

> ("For a coffin I want a sarape,
> for a cross my cartridge belts,
> and as they write upon my tomb,
> my last goodbye with a thousand bullets,
> ay, ay, honey, why don't you love me?"
>
> 'The Bed of Stone,' Cuco Sánchez)

For a coffin I want a wool blanket
to shield me from the ground and sky,
so I can feel the breath of the earth,
or the breeze of the heavens
touching and cooling my body.

I have a Spanish army blanket,
brown and white like the hills of Castile,
after years of wear, still stiff.
How many young men have lain with it,
shivering like children,
only relieved with cold light
mixing its milk into dawn's sky?
Do they still carry
its memory?

I have a Mexican sarape,
with magic yellow birds.
It's my daughter's love, her embrace.

Its thinning weave brings me
a young woman's warmth
and I know she knows.
It's a mother's touch
spinning the yarn,
it's the wrapped old men in the plaza,
a caress of the first sun on their
     shoulders,
and the confidence of a young hawker
in the market
on a cold Sunday morning.

I have a store-bought blanket,
pink and light green.
The satin edge is worn
by chins and necks,
by hidden young love,
grandchildren's feet
and a lonesome old woman
who slept with her cat.

The honor of blankets sacred to life,
passed to me by my father,
by my mother,
from the Rastro, the marketplace,
the sale of an estate . . .
I need one,
any one will do,
that I can carry with me.

THE PASS, April, 1957 (For my brother Dennis)

Cool dawn
and an open road
had awakened in my father
a comfort of speed
—only achieved
when my mother
was not along—
dropping down from the
mountains
onto the high Toluca plain
on our way
to Valle de Bravo's
"Circuito de Avándaro,"
where the young Rodríguez
brothers
were going to race.

A silver-gray
Ferrari roadster
#11 on the door
passed us
with a startling bump
of air
pulling back into the lane
far ahead
down the road.
The driver wore coveralls
and a black knit hat
hands at 8 and 4
on a large wooden wheel—
his head held steady

in fresh buffets
of early morning
Mexican air.

The pass
was perfect.

John Von Neumann.

We'd been passed
by a star.

I can still see
the caressing
trajectory of the
Testarrosa.

I can still hear
roadsound
in the curved metal
bulkheads and fenders.

I can still feel
mineral warmth
pumping through
the aluminum motor veins
that he felt that morning.

I hold
the wheel

at 8 and 4
enjoying the heat
held down
around my feet
by the cool air
pushing incessantly
at the back of my collar
and feel
a tap of air
off the front
of a truck I pass—
headed to school
on a wonderful
spring day.

He lapped the field.

John von Neumann exits the corkscrew at Laguna Seca in his Ferrari 625 TRC, November 1957. Photo credit, Michael T. Lynch Archive

NASCAR (Pennsylvania 500 at POCONO)

> To: Governor Tom Ridge of Pennsylvania, giving a guest politician's dull monotone delivery of the command, "Gentlemen, - start - your - engines," at the start of the Pennsylvania 500 at Pocono—
>
> From: The young freckle-shouldered man on my right, wearing an old black Darrell Waltrip tank top, holding his second half-quart of Bud—
>
> "He just doesn't fucking get it, does he."

It's a gathering
of Americans
from New York,
Boston, Rochester and
the South,
an uncountable crowd
of over one hundred thousand,
come to celebrate
the thrill of freedom
we feel in working,
saving up
for a car,
settling into the seat
and sensing the weight
of driving a steady 70,
tank after tank of gas,
across the country
on the Eisenhower
Interstate System.

We come in a

brotherhood
and sisterhood
of things we know
how to use
every day—
tobacco, beer, furniture,
guns, candy, pop
and soap—
gas, oil, Ford, Pontiac,
and Chevrolet.

And we come
to worship
our gods
of the open road—
Dick, Darrell, Jeff,
Dale, John, Bill,
Jimmie and Rusty,
Kenny and Mike—
who, like us,
have the same
names,
and who, like us,
come from
hometowns
no one
outside the family
has ever heard of—
Chemung, Kannapolis, Hueytown,
Batesville, Owensboro, Pittsboro,
Spanaway, Dawsonville,
Fenton and Randleman.

We come
in a uniform of caps,
and T-shirts
to sing
with the soul
of the full-bodied
American
carburated V8,
and to hoist
our rebel civilization
up to the whole world's
broad sky,
and we flip the finger
to sissy
computer-enhanced
thrills
and to those who
just don't understand
the tradition
of outrunning the law.

We come to celebrate
our country's ways—
R and D in a smudged
spiral notebook,
Terry and Bobby's
proud mother
signing her autograph
in the pits,
and men
great enough
to thank the Lord
for winning

a race and then
dance
destruction
into the roof of
their car.

NASCAR racing
is the common poetry
of hardworking
America's
industrial and
corporate roar,
that lets
each of us live
the tingling thrill
of being one
in a river of many,
swirling around together
with deafening power.

COUNTRY SUNDAY

(near Bethune, South Carolina,
driving back to Atlanta from the
Rockingham race)

An old man
and a little boy,
dressed in Sunday clothes,
walking
a South Carolina road—
they're a mile or more from town
—seems like nowhere—
whe're they goin'?

going home
going home

The old man's got
a high-crowned cap
and the little boy
pulls on his hand
trying to lean out
toward the road—
I pull left a bit
not to get too close

going home
going home

And he tips his hat
to give me thanks—

—the Carolina road
glitters with bits of quartz,
shining green-mown grass
along each side
—autumn leaves
glow with gold and rust
this Sunday evening
as far as we can see . . .

going home
going home

A MAN (for Dan S.)

There is
a man who works
in the university cafeteria
about forty or so
that I see
nearly every day
picking up trays
left on the tables.
He always wears
the same outfit—
plain blue pants,
short-sleeved shirt,
straight across the bottom,
never tucked in—
a taste in clothes
that shows
preference for
a monotone
worn by those
who have stayed
in the background
for years.

I've always known
that he was one of those,
since the university
kindly hires
some who need hiring.

He keeps
his brown hair cut

like a useful brush,
and walks
in constant lines
and time.

I have never seen him
show a smile—
he has that set frown
that reminds us
that nature,
in the grandeur
of its cliffs
and crevasses,
doesn't think
that way.

I've run into
the man twice
in recent days
in new places—
once at a bus stop
in Spokane,
and this evening
riding my bike
to the store.

Something
about his world
clearly
and quietly
is telling me
about where I'm going
in mine.

And tonight—
as I saw him
standing
in front of a
one-man
brick house
on South Grand—
I finally know—

His success
is in his agreement
with the world—
his art
in the uniformly
arranged
pink petunias
by his sidewalk
that he waters
each evening
holding a hose.

A PHOTOGRAPH OF ZAPATA

I cleaned up the walls
of my office today.
It was time
for a change.
I gave away an Audubon print
of a redwing blackbird,
threw out a poster of Einstein,
and took down
cluttered quotes
from Sophocles, Shakespeare,
Borges, Montaigne
and Frost.
I don't need to proclaim my being
through them right now.

But I am keeping
the picture post card
of Emiliano Zapata
sitting next to
Pancho Villa
in the gilded chairs
in President Carranza's office,
whom they had just run out
of Mexico City . . .

A crowd of men breathing
warm tequila air

in the president's office

The weight of wide hats,
matted black hair

in the president's office

Hands used to holding
pistols and reins

in the president's office

Perfumed silk suits
mixed with bullets and spurs

in the president's office

and Zapata's eyes,
obsidian eyes,
cat eyes prowling
the Morelos canefields,
eyes that still terrify and freeze
those who nervously
shuffle through papers
and plans,

in the president's office

Francisco "Pancho" Villa and Emiliano Zapata in
President Carranza's office, November, 1914
Photo credit *Mutual Film Company*

FRIENDS (for Larry Deaver and Jeff Duenwald)

I live in a world
where men
take their dreams
and walk them for miles
across the land.

Others
only see
such journeys
on a map,
in a photograph,
or wonder
about them
in a book.

Others have never
stood
on a ridge
and dared to breathe
the beauty
of the air of death
and of life
at the same time.

The men I know
tell their stories
without a trace
of boasting,
because they have seen
the truth
of the world.

The men I know
often become silent
reflecting
on the gravity
of life they see
in their ancestors,
in themselves,
their children,
their wives,
their lovers.

They are men
whose names
are honored
with the vast echoes
of time
in the great mountains . . .
We meet in places
where the icy air
makes the outline
of our being
clear.

Author, and Steve Jeffries, West Rib Mt. Mckinley. Photo, Matt Chase

LOVE

I watched
Ralph Emery
interview
Loretta Lynn.
They are both
getting old.
They both
color their hair.
Loreta is showing
more teeth
than ever.
They talked about
the usual—
how she got started
in Blaine and Puyallup,
Washington,
her successful songs,
the "Coal Miner's Daughter" film,
and pitched
her new gospel CD
sold only by mail.
Ralph and Loretta
are old
showbiz friends
who TV-touch each other
on the arm
and say "I love you."
But then
she began
remembering
tiny details

of the day
Patsy Cline
was killed.

Then she recounted
running between
one floor and
the other
of the hospital
where both
her husband
and Conway Twitty
were dying,
and that the last time
Conway was gone,
but still warm.

Then Buck Owens,
who gave her
her first job
on the radio,
came on
by video hookup
from Bakersfield,
and they talked
some more.
At the very end
he said,
"You know,
I've never told this
to a soul,
but
I've had a crush

on you since
we first met
in Tacoma
in 1960 . . . "

They all tried
to make light
of it
in the usual ways.

But it stuck.

DOC (1989-2005)

I had to wait
so long, so long,
to get the dog
I was expecting
in 1950.
I have no idea
why I really expected
a dog
for my birthday.
It was child
logic.
My father's best friend
had a dog
that dad liked
to play with.
I didn't know
that my father's joy
was not really the dog,
but George.
So when
my older brother
got excited about
my birthday
I just knew.
(I completely missed
my mother's silence
that I can still hear
until this day).
And when they all
said come down to
the garage,

I knew that dogs
were kept
in the garage.

A bicycle.

I learned to
ride it, but I
remember the dog
much better.

And now
I still remember,
whenever my dog,
MY DOG
greets ME,
bounding out
of the garage,
or wishes, so fervently
that I will take him
with me.
His dog logic
seems very familiar.
He is
that timeless dog
sent with
the same joy,
the same luck,
that finally makes me
a boy and his dog.

Doc and me, North Idaho backcountry.
Photo by Denny Burmeister

THE CANTABRIAN SEA

The pretty
young mothers
push their babies
in strollers
along the breakwater
in Llanes.

And while
they pause
to visit,
the children
are silent.
But they are not
sleeping.

They are listening
with astonished eyes
to the heavy
hissing waves
breathe
in and out
of the gray
limestone
headlands.

Don't their mothers know
how dangerous it is

to hold a child
too close
to a place
where the earth
meets the sea?

FOR THERESA PUTHOFF (on her birthday)

In 324 B.C.
Alexander the Great
married a desert princess
he had met
on his journey of conquest
through central Asia.
He said he had found
the most beautiful woman
in the world.

I have often wondered
what she was like.

Alexander was
one of Aristotle's
favorite students.
It was no surprise
to the great philospher
and scientist
that Alexander
had become so wise a leader
of his father's empire
as such a young man.

I wonder why he said
she was so fascinating
compared to the host
of beautiful Greeks

and Macedonians
he knew,
and if he ever talked
about women
with his famous teacher.

He found her in
one of the widest deserts
of the world.
They didn't speak
the same language.
He said at first
she didn't want to leave,
she loved the life
of breaking camp,
riding all day,
and caring for
horses, camels
and children
in the sand.

I wonder what
the most powerful man
in the world
did to make her
change her mind.

We know about
Alexander's territorial
conquests
from the great historians

of the ages.

Anything we know about his wife
comes from his own few
recorded words.

He said she had
amazing eyes.

VALENTINE'S DAY

It started
with dimestore cards
or cut-out paper hearts
we'd put in "mailboxes"
at each others' desks

and then we'd count them up
and hope we got the one
we really wanted

Then
we learned to buy
a serious card
and enclose
some little heart-shaped candies
with clever, silly sayings

imitating what we thought
grown-up love was all about

And later
came dinners out
in candlelight
with memories sweetened
by fancy desserts

And so today
as I bit into a frosted sugar cookie
heart

and let a bon bon spread its
overwhelming
chocolate flood
across my tongue

I thought that all the
cookies,
cut-outs,
cards and bouquets
were really just lines of today's
poem
about the amazing
soft touch of sunlight
somewhere on your rose-petal
skin.

MIDWAY DIRECT (for my daughter Shelley on her 31st birthday)

    I can hardly hear you
    over the sound
    of the river below . . .

    Swallows and salmon
    come up the canyon,
    come back to your home
    every year.

    I feel you answer
    my two firm tugs
    with two of your own,
    and as I begin
    to take up the rope
    I know
    that you surely know.

    Swallows and salmon
    come up the canyon,
    come back to your home
    every year.

    The rope—with the cool weight
    of a braid—
    tells my hands
    you are now passing spots
    where I paused to see
    which way was best.
    You have followed the crack,
    stepped out left to traverse,

and then onto a knobby, high
face.

Swallows and salmon
come up the canyon,
come back to your home
every year.

Occasionally
I see your white helmet
leaning out
to see where you're going,
and I begin to hear
the exhilarating aluminum
mountain music
of the hardware
you are collecting
as you come.

Swallows and salmon
come up the canyon
come back to your home
every year.

Then I see your outline
clearly formed and filled
with your own
pleasure and grace
on the curved slab of granite,
swallows around you,
against the breathtaking drop
to the river . . .
the river that you and I

will always hear
below.

*Swallows and salmon
come up the canyon,
come back to your home
every year*

Summit Mt. Rainier, Shelley Higman, Perry Higman.
Photo by Tom Couraud

FOR JESSE (my son, hurt in a car crash, 1983)

Here is
what you and I
have learned.

Like Hercules,
Achilles, and Ulysses,
you were tested early.
You could not
run away
and so you fought—
you grasped death
by the arm
and felt

as they still feel

the sharp edge of existence
cut your flesh,
and you know

as they still know

that the stare
of death
is a mirror
of our own
living eyes,
granting us
the clear outline
of a story
or song

to be heard
and remembered
as theirs is still sung

You have entered
a solitary world
where few have walked
—where the only men you meet
are heroes—
and you have discovered
the awe
of your own great soul.

And you know that alone
in the desert night,
your tiny being
fills
the timeless space
between the earth
and the stars.

Jesse, *Danny Clinch Photography.* Dannyclinch.com

ART (for Jesse and Shelley)

> "Not one of us could paint like that..."
>
> Attributed to Pablo Picasso, upon
> seeing the cave paintings in Altamira.

We were
alone
with the guardián
in the long
limestone
Cueva de El Pindal
in a ravine
looking over
the rainy
Cantabrian Sea.

"They lived
out front
in the 'vestibule,'
and painted
deep inside
where there is
no light."

With a hand-
lantern
we saw
the groupings—
chamois, bison,
horses, reindeer,
on a rock flake,
rows of even dots,

a painted
left hand,
a mammoth,
red vertical lines
marking an
overhanging
edge.
"They are
not realistic
like photographs.
They are
symbolic
of the ritual
importance
of certain
animals."

The meltwater
from the ice
is still
dripping shapes
into the caverns
where we walk.

And as I exhale
a momentary
steadying breath
held
since the ages
of glaciers,
I can feel
in the weight

of my left forearm
how it is
to stroke
in paint
the perfect curve
of the crest
on the back
of a bison.

Shelley Higman, Rome. Photo by Jesse Higman

ROY ROGERS & ME (on the news of Roy Rogers' death)

>I was thinking
>just a day or two ago
>about rolling up
>the cuff
>of my jeans.
>I thought that today's styles
>needed a lift.
>
>I was thinking
>just a day or two ago
>about my righteous
>tonguelashing of colleagues
>who had assumed
>I would be passive
>if they attacked
>a weaker person.
>I thought
>they clearly needed
>to learn a lesson.
>
>I was thinking
>just a day or two ago
>about the luck
>of having a friend to admire,
>of knowing a good horse,
>and sharing with them
>the squint
>of bright eyes
>and a plain smile.

I was thinking
just a day or two ago,
that I wish everyone
could have the chance
to feel what it's like
to be somebody
and tip a fine hat
to a lady.

I was thinking
just a day or two ago
about the cool
morning freshness
in American
Western music,
the peaceful
echoes in
its sounds
that come to me
in the mountains
and deserts of the West.

I was thinking
just a day or two ago
that more of us
need to feel
those parts
of our soul.

MT. ADAMS (July 12, 3:50 A.M.)

There is a time
of dawn
before light comes
when I'm headed
up the trail . . .
and in my solitary steps
I am with
all the others.

The night
holds us all
as we imagine
first light.

I am with
George Mallory
who lay awake
with his own
breath and heartbeat,
Everest's awesome
circle of night
overpowering . . .
and knowing
he can go higher,
is drawn relentlessly
by the great mountain's gravity
upward
to find
his life.

I am with
Ulysses
hearing the wind
come up in the night,
and quickening waves
against the lapped sides
of his boat.
Light will bring
his men back to him.
Then together,
pushing the bow
from the beach,
the sea-worn hull
will again ride
water and time,
and they can clearly face
their search for home.

I am with
my grandfather Paul
who learned to work
to provide.
Light will reveal
to him comfort
of strong coffee
and the morning jobs
awaiting
in his shop
where
he can keep
a precise
tiny world

of gears and shafts
in perfect motion.
With night again,
he'll go alone
to the symphony,
but the music
will only soothe him . . .
not make him dream.

Faint light
and I see
I am alone—
when a deer
and I meet—
each form present,
equally surprised.
He has been
with his spirits, too.
We think
for a moment
we do not know
each other.
But both hearts
jumping together,
we realize
we are both alive.

We each go our own way
in the eternal dawn.

HOLDING SYDNEY

> "the stars in the sky look down where he lay,
> the little Lord Jesus asleep in the hay . . . "
>
> John McFarland / James Murray / Tammy Wynette

At Christmastime
Curt and I
were on a climbing trip.
We had been
many nights
close to the stars
on the volcanoes
of Mexico.

On top
of Citlaltépetl,
we wondered
aloud
if the child
had yet
been born.

Back in Spokane
one of the first
things
was to see her.
Others
already had come,
seen Sydney
in her crib,

the stuffed animals
watching
from the shelf
above.

Barbara
welcomed me
in the kitchen,
still showing
celestial surprise
in her soft,
tired,
brown eyes.

She said,
"Do you want
to hold her?"

As I cradled Sydney
the slight
but unmistakable
touch
of her soul
settled down
like snow
onto my shoulders
—with about
the same weight
as an angel.

And as
I felt

her warmth
sink quietly
into the muscle
of my left arm,
and she looked
peacefully
around me
toward the world,
we carried each other
into our own
memories
of the endlessly
rolling universe.

Sydney Chase, age 14. Photo by Barb Chase

THE VIETNAM VETERANS MEMORIAL (for Matt Chase)

> "Give ear, my friends, amid your sufferings, to words that I shall say. We cannot here know which way lies the west, nor where the east, nor where the the sun, that shines for all mankind, descends below the earth, now where again he rises from it."
>
> Odysseus in, *The Odyssey*, (W. C. Bryant trans.)

We walked down
into the summer night
looking for
your father
on the wall,
and
in the deepest place,
the middle fold,
carved in black granite,
we found the name
Mark Richardson Chase.

Together,
in the space
around his name
and the others',
we slowly entered
the dark weather
of dreams
and we knew
that our names, too,
and our blood
and our time

fluttered
the same
as the white letters

like snowflakes

in the names
on the wall.

I spread my hand
on the warm stone
and felt the shoulders
of Hartill, Ronca,
Williams, McDonald, Starley,
Wynn, Meyerkord, Rose, Lagerwall
—and Chase—
and looked into the stars
of the Washington, D.C. sky.

Photo, Shelley Higman

LINES FROM MY FATHER'S SONG (On hearing of Lloyd Anderson's death)

> "Such men
> I never saw, nor shall I see again, --
> men like Pirithous and like Druas, lord
> of nations, Caeneus and Exadius,
> and the great Polypheme, and Theseus, son
> of Aegeus, likest to the immmortal gods."
>
>   Nestor, in <u>The Iliad</u> (W. C. Bryant trans.)

The names I heard my father read
were Mummery, Mallory
and Irvine, Norton, Somervell,
Harrer,
Herzog, Terray, Rebuffat,
and the names of friends he spoke
were Bauer, Ulrichs, Grage and Alt,
MacGowan,
and Anderson.

    I want my father to know
    that I haven't forgotten,
    and that my son
    and my daughter
    have heard the names
    too.

    I want my father to know
    that I've found some of my places
    in his places, and in theirs,

and that I have heard the lines of
his song
in Alaska, Scotland,
Wales, Mexico,
in Chamonix,
and South America,
on the glacier ice
of Mount Rainier,
and on the granite faces
of the High Sierra,
the Tetons, Sawtooths
and North Cascades.

I want my father to know
that I'm still singing the songs,
and others now too:
Beckey,
the Whittaker brothers,
Schoening and Roskelley,
Messner and Lowe,
and my friends
States, Duenwald, and Deaver,
Jeffries, Curtis, and Hanson,
Burmeister, Bishop,
and Chase.

I last saw Lloyd Anderson
on a bright September day,
gazing out a window
at the breezy blue water
of Puget Sound.

He rose from the couch,
grasped my hand
until my knuckles popped

(he thought I was you, Dad)

and said, "See, Chester,
I wanted you to know
that I still have a little strength
left."

He was 96 years old.

Chet Higman, Pinnacle Peak, 1936. Photo by Bea Kauffman

UNOPENED GIFTS

> "Gracias quiero dar . . .
> por la música, misteriosa forma del
> tiempo."
>
> ("I want to give thanks for music,
> a mysterious form of time.")
>
> from, 'Otro poema de los dones,' 'Another
> poem of gifts'
>
> Jorge Luis Borges

While she played
the single slow notes
of a night melody
from the New World Symphony
on her recorder,
my mother
made us row out
in Liberty Bay
and look up
at the Milky Way

waiting

on the black water
to see a fish stir
the phosphorescence,
or hear a seal
blow out a breath
after gliding like an owl

through his mysterious
liquid sky.

The steady dipping of the oars
is still my pace,
my comfort is
knowing I belong

to the sea
and the stars.

HAWAIIAN CHRISTMAS SURFER

A Christmas dawn Hawaiian surfer
stands solid on a wave,
long paddle in his hand just like
a shepherd's staff.

The skies last night
were shot with stars
to praise the magic Birth,
and he is out this glorious day
to ride the magic surf.

As he gazes to the eastern sky
across the planet's curving face,
he knows that new and sacred Life
comes with the sun each day.

He rides this holy morn' in grace,
like an old Hawaiian hymn,
as the glory of the ancient waves
spread power into him.

When two thousand years ago the gale
dashed the boat on Galilee
our Lord walked to it through the storm
—a miracle of faith.

But the miracle I witness here today
this dawning Christmas day,
is that He is constantly reborn
in the joy the Christmas morning surfer feels,
walking on the waves.

LILIES ON THE DAY OF OUR HOLY VIRGIN OF GUADALUPE
(for Bardomiano Balbuena)

I have
always loved
Diego Rivera's
"Flower Vendors"—
yellow-white lilies
and Mexican women's
brown skin.

I drove
into Valle de Bravo
after forty years
and walked
to my old fishing spot
along the same lake.
I saw
burros
and a horse
turn up
the Calle de la Culebra
toward
Sr. Balbuena's house.
I went
to the falls
on the river
we'd cross
every day
—it was still
flowing,
mist still

rising.

I wish
he were here
to send me
to the market
to buy Alcohol
and orange juice
for his day off,
or tell me
"vamos
a la pesca,"
so I could
go to the lake
with the best
fisherman
in town.

As I
rounded
a corner
to go
to my car,
a small country
woman
in worn
white
cotton clothes,
cradling
a full
armload
of lilies

looked into
my eyes
with a smile.

The lilies
were real.

Bardomiano Balbuena (in hat), wife, child. Photo by Bea Higman

BUTTERFLY

My eyes
were drawn up
to see
the constant blue
Guadalajara skies,

And I saw
a butterfly
—a floating
black and yellow
flower—
and watched
it bump
the shiny
reflective glass

dark as obsidian—
blue-green as jade—

of the new
University
Graduate School
Building.
It tapped
along
several panes
and fluttered

softly away.

It knew
the Mexican sky
could turn
to stone.

MEETING IN MADRID (March 12, 2004)

    We meet in Madrid
    the morning after Atocha.
    The bombers think
    we are different now.

    But I find I am at home
    watching Velázquez' young Bacchus
    on the street with the drunks,
    Rubens' three goddesses
    posing for Paris,
    and Bosch's look into
    our strange delights
    and hells.

VIEW FROM ANETO (SPANISH PYRENEES)
A tribute to Charles Martel, Pelayo, Roland, and Charlemagne

    I've been to Covadonga.
    Pelayo's cave is dark
    and dripping water.
    I've been to Roncesvalles,
    when heavy snow in spring
    still filled the pass.
    I've been to Aragón
    where cliffs string out
    whole rivers into threads.

    The desert men,
    whose abstract Allah
    would never tolerate
    such blatant contension,
    could go no further.

Aneto, Spanish Pyrenees, Kate Schertenlieb, Denny Burmeister, Perry Higman. Photo by Denny Burmeister

BAPTISM (on a bicycle pilgrimage from Spokane to Chimayó, New Mexico)

>I was baptized
>today.
>I swung
>my naked body weight
>under a heavy plank
>sheep bridge,
>willows and sagebrush
>hushing the sight,
>and sat
>in the heavenly ice-
>water of the high
>Lemhi River.
>To the polite
>applause of the stream
>and softly ringing
>sheepbells
>I washed
>and became
>mountain clean.
>
>I rose
>and could sense
>the joyous paths
>of swallows above
>and knew the sun
>was deliberately
>warming
>my soul.

THE MAIL (in Dove Creek, Colorado)

Riding into the foothills
of the Southern Rockies
I passed a man
walking
down his driveway
to the mailbox—
green lawn
on both sides.

Each step
was a moment
of his morning.

I want
to live
long enough
to know
what it's like
to plan for the mail,
for my arms
to get thin,
and to hear
every small note
of the mountain
chickadee.

ON THE SHOULDER OF HIGHWAY 93 (South of Stevensville, Montana)

Last year
I drove by
an older farm couple
loading a power mower
into their pickup
on the shoulder
of highway 93

and quickly
I passed them
so quickly at sixty
but I saw
what was going on

They had just done
their weekly mowing
to keep the grass
and the sadness
from growing
around a white cross
with ribbons and flowers
on the shoulder
of highway 93

I wonder
this summer
when I drive
the same road

if I will notice
mown grass
or just see
a faded white cross
along the shoulder
of highway 93

And I wonder
who will tend
to the memories
the couple will leave
as their summers roll on
into fall

for quickly
so quickly
at sixty
a turn of the highway
or seasons
can change it all

HOMESTEAD (near Douglas, Washington)

Two old cottonwoods
some lilacs
and a row of Russian olives
are all that remains
of a farm
that's gone away.

Somewhere
sits an old woman
in the summer shade
remembering
in the song of a meadowlark,

maybe near,
maybe far

the weight of water carried
in metal pails,
the hot wind's rush
at her bare ankles,
the scratch of grasshoppers
in yellow leaves that blow,
before the bones of trees
begin to show.

FIRST RAIN

> "Las primeras gotas fueron
> las de un fuerte chaparrón,
> las que al caer en mi sombrero
> alegran mi corazón,
> ay la la lay, mi corazón . . . "
>
> ("The first big drops that fell
> announced the coming rain,
> and as I heard them hit my hat
> my heart began to sing,
> ay la la lay,
> my heart began to sing . . . ")
>
>   'El aguacero,' 'Thunderstorm,'
>
>   Tomás Méndez / Miguel
>   Aceves Mejía

After sixty-three days of sun
a rainsquall reminds us
that we are made of earth
and sky.

The dust
billowing up
wetted by the big drops first

stirs the same dirt smells
that gave to God the idea
for living things . . .

and breathes into us
the breath
of life.

PLACES AND MEN

*I am called
from the past
by men
and the places
we have been.*

I have
a picture postcard
showing
the rock walls
on Silver Star Peak
Hermann Ulrichs sent
to my grandfather Harry.
My mother said
Hermann traveled
the world on his own
and when he was here
he'd come over
and play Rachmaninoff
on the piano
and bounce me
on his knee.
He climbed
Silver Star alone.
So did I.

*I am here
and I remember.*

Glenn Fulton
treated me
like a ranch hand,
and never let me know
I was only fourteen.
I sat silently beside him
going 100 mph
in a dusty Mercury sedan,
and I learned to read
the space
between a horse
and a cow
—following him
to a place
I could live
in a cowboy's mind.

*I am here
and I remember.*

I sailed the Aegean
in the sharp winds
of May,
and many times
crossed the wake
of Odysseus
and his men
out of sight
of land.
Home
was a horizon

of waves
that made
my longing
for you
stronger.

*I am here
and I remember.*

There is a time
in our lives
when we are
at our best—
when we reach
a finish
polished by our skills.

So when
they found
George Mallory
still on Mt. Everest,
I saw
in the white stone strength
of his monumental back
the power
of loneliness
in my soul.

*I am called
from the past
and I remember.*

ONE

> " . . . here a single deed has room . . . "
> Walt Whitman

A meadowlark
sings his single song
that echoes off the sun
and fills the prairie space

A coyote
sings his single song
that echoes off the moon
and fills a lonely place

A cowboy
sings his single song
a yodeled prayer
beneath God's starry heavens
to guide him to a mate

ANGEL

> "Let brotherly love continue.
>
> Be not forgetful to entertain strangers: for thereby some have entertained angels unawares."
>
> Hebrews 13: 1, 2 (KJV)

My guardian angel
hangs around a lot
these days,
and to tell the truth
I'll bet he always has.
I think my mother and father
knew about him
when I was just a baby,
and before I was born, maybe,
and then, when I was
growing up.

He is that angel
the little Lord Jesus
first sent to me
in the Christmas song
many years ago
to keep me from feeling lonely,
yet brings me the beauty
of more loneliness
and more tears
as I grow older.

He is an angel
real as the toy rabbit or duck
that sits looking at me
on the dash of my car
as we take our journeys,
or real as the life that exists
within framed photographs on my
desk.

He is that angel
who firmly takes my hand
and makes us take a daring step
to open and brilliant,
almost always windy places,
where he and I clearly see
what we can create.

He is that angel
who whispers my secrets
to others I love
sweetly guiding them
to fill their love
in loving me.

Now I realize
he is an angel
who smiles gently as he tiptoes by
pretending to be unseen,
as a child hides from his mother or
father,

when in fact his powerful
presence
carries God's thunder.

He is that angel
that I smile with now
when yet again he shows me
we are witness to great mysteries
—music singing just for me,
and him . . . and her . . . —
and all the other simple beings
floating gloriously for just an
instant
together.

And he is the angel
I pray will stay with me every day
even when I'm gone away.

PINESMOKE

> "Hard times are real,
> there's dusty fields
> no matter where you go . . . "
>
> 'Where Corn Don't Grow,'
>
> Roger Murrah / Mark Allen
> Springer / Travis Tritt

I still know the country
and sometimes I go.

I'm back where smells
of pinesmoke, cattle, horses,
garbage burning, and sounds
of cars on the road,
dogs barking, frogs,
and june bugs,
all lived in the distance
and tried to fill the silence.

It may be the purest
nostalgia.
The work and pain,
sensual loneliness,
were all real,
like the echo of a meadowlark
in open spaces.

The author shoeing near Cheney, Washington, 1980.
Photo by Bea Higman

HEROES

> ". . . pistola en mano se le echaban de a montón.
> 'Estoy borracho,' les gritaba, 'y soy buen gallo,' cuando una bala atravesó su corazón."
>
> (". . . he drew his pistol as they fell upon him. 'I'm drunk,' he shouted, 'and I'm a real rooster,' when a bullet went clean through his heart.")
>
>   'Juan Charrasqueado,'
>
>   Victor Cordero / Jorge Negrete

I need to know about my heroes.
John Wayne played John Bernard Books,
an aging gunfighter, with a cancer
who decided to die
in a hail of bullets, taking out three old
enemies. Wayne was at the time
dying of cancer.
I want to know
from someone who was there
who knows.
Was he scared or
did he pass his courage on to his family
at the very last minute?
He played the part, how
could he do that? Or did he?

Did Negrete go like Juan, "drunk enough
so he didn't feel the bullets?"
Did he look right at, no blindfold,

spit at the rifles,
look right into the face of death with his
own colder eyes that said,
"and . . . ?"

Will Robert Duvall think about Gus?
Has it "been quite a party?"
Will he drift off, with pride unbroken?
What does that mean to him?

Will I be my life, my art,
still trying to become myself? Or
will I play someone else?

USS ARIZONA MEMORIAL

While I've walked many roads above you
you've lived your life beneath the waves,
I know we keep growing closer,
for my pathway narrows now with age.

You who died your first War-day
while I was born and stayed for years
have seen each other time to time
through the sadness of our tears,

In fields around Gettysburg,
in France and Texas and in Spain,
and on a western prairie hill
where all who rode in pride remain.

And whether flags in rows of crosses,
plain grasses blowing, or the oil thread
that ties me to your ship below,

they tell the story we both know—
that you and I will meet the others
where we're bound to go

THE FINAL STEP (for Carmen, at the death of his daughter Alexa)

>Choices narrow
>and now I hold
>between one hand
>and the other
>this mountain's final tower
>
>beneath my heels
>—only toes on ledges—
>a deep stream
>of granite crystals
>falls away
>to earth below
>
>and knowing
>I have reached the edges
>of the final step,
>above me
>in endless blue
>I see
>
>shiny like a starlit night
>a raven roll in his delight
>
>and he tells me

"Yes, I know about Alexa,

she is well.

And I know about you, too"

THE TOUCH OF THE EARTH

As a boy
my favorite toys
were dumptrucks
and bulldozers.
I still recall
the sounds they made,
and wiping
the warm smell
of dirt
from under my nose
with the back
of my hand
as I played.

*I remember
the touch of the earth.*

In grade school
ball games
I loved to slide into base,
so I could stand up
and shake
the hard-earned honor
of dirt from my pants,
or rub my hands
in dust and spit
to hold the bat.

I remember

the touch of the earth.

In time
I began to believe in
the warm power of a horse
—his sweat and mine
mixed in the rising dust
of distance covered
on a long day's ride.

I remember
the touch of the earth.

Later I learned
the fertile sound
of dampened dirt,
cut, turned
and dropped from
the moldboards of a plow
pulling through sod
on a cool summer morning.

I remember
the touch of the earth.

As a man
I've buried calves and colts,
dogs and cats,
poured out
family ashes
on mountain ridges

where the sacred
dirt and dust of death
stuck conspicuously
to my boots.

*I remember
the touch of the earth.*

I've breathed dust
—been bathed in mud.
I've bitten dirt
between my teeth,
I've dug its grit
beneath my nails.

But now
when I cannot touch the earth
I miss it,
and I know I'll kiss it
crying
when I come home.

I remember.

I know.

I already know

*the touch
of the earth.*

THANK YOU SONG TO A COWBOY (for Deb Copenhaver)

Thanks

to Bardomiano Balbuena, Mexican woodcutter, who taught me to feed the burros first, after a hard day's work

to Billy Smith, Papago cowboy, who took me to Nogales, bought me a guitar, and showed me some chords

to my father, Chester, who told me in a secret moment that his favorite song was Gene Autry's 'Red River Valley'

to Glenn Fulton, central Oregon rancher, who sent me alone into the mountains on a horse to bring in cows and calves

to mythical gaucho don Segundo Sombra—in his shadow on the Pampas I found myself "longing for the horizon"

to Buck Owens, for taking the time to tell me he grew up with Mexican country music

to Willie Nelson, who already wrote and sang this song

and thanks to you, Deb, for teaching
me that the words and music are true

Deb Copenhaver being recognized by the crowd at National Finals Rodeo, 2010. Photo, Molly Morrow *Molly Morrow Photography*, Ellensburg, Washington. Mollymorrow.com

PILLOWS

I've slept with my head on a saddle,
I've slept with my head on a pack
I've slept with my head on my shirt and my pants
and I've slept with a pillow in bed.

These are the things that have held me in sleep,
and kept my black night-thoughts in check
the smell of their breath whispers my story
and I know they'll still hold me in death.

IOWA

In October of 1966
Sandra and I
walked into a cornfield
where we found
the wide weight
of muddy midwest rivers,
fireflies in the brush
after dark,
rainfall
in blinding sheets,
lightning enough
to light the cities
of heaven,
and deep earth
that grows and grows
and grows.

And so
the drying leaves of corn
still hold us
and remind us
to follow their music
through all of our seasons.

SANDRA AT SIXTY

In old black and white photographs
I know the little girl
playing in silence with her dolls,
looking out over the sea

baby, daughter,
schoolgirl,
woman, lover,
mother,
come and walk the world
with me

I can see you still
with all the other
pretty women,
scarves and skirts
—a rush like an eager
mountain stream—
in downtown Boston
city streets

baby, daughter,
schoolgirl,
woman, lover,
mother,
come and walk the world
with me

Across a room

in Iowa City I saw you
dressed in a blue and white
ocean wave
—and found that once kissed
by the ocean I could never leave—

baby, daughter,
schoolgirl,
woman, lover,
mother,
come and walk the world
with me

And I see you now
in the garden at sixty,
birds reveling in the bushes,
and plants jostling and crowding
with their leaves
to touch your sunlit skin,
and the earth sighing
each time you run your fingers
through its warm hair . . .

baby, daughter,
schoolgirl,
woman, lover,
mother,
come, come, come, and walk the
world with me

   (with thanks to Heather Nova)

KONA NIGHT

The doves had settled
and were cooing soft
as cotton
—you on your side
and I on my side of the bed—
only clothing made a whisper
like feathers falling,
while between us breathed
a longing,
like the weather has
to roam the world
and comb the darkness
of the night.

Startling curves
of white
dark silhouettes of tan
I touched them once
I touched them twice
and you spoke,

"yes, that's right."

In dreams I sailed
the seas on easy breezes,
then through storms
of rain and lightning
while traveling over

all the stones
we've known
in life . . .

it was a dove
who brought to me
the message of
the morning light.

AFTER A RAIN

I had forgotten
after a rain
half-grown green corn
and how
it reaches deeper each moment
a tiny stream of water
guided down every stalk
by the leaves
into the dirt
row after row after row
as the storm blows east
out of Iowa.

And then
in the dampened night

when most of the secret growing
takes place

how fireflies rise
in silent primitive blinking
and show the celebration
of Earth's love
to the stars.

DEATH WILL COME TO ME

> "Ponme mi vestido blanco,
> aquél con que nos casamos . . . "
>
> ("Dress me in my white clothes,
> the ones we got married in . . .")
>
> from, 'Tata Dios,' 'Papa God'
> Valeriano Trejo / Miguel Aceves Mejía

You will come to me
in a white dress, bright
and plain,
and on its curves and folds
I will be able to read all the years,
what we created together,
and those terrible moments
we both prayed we could take back.

I will know
that I must follow on,
yet one last time
you will allow me your hand,
always offered in peace,
and I will again feel
the living glow
of your hip and thigh.

For a moment
we will linger and be

both young and old—
and then
when your light strikes me
from all directions
and shadows vanish
I will breathe in relief
of being in your beauty
and take my final bold step
forward.

Credits:

"Others may praise what they like . . ." Walt Whitman, 1891

"La cama de piedra"©1953, José del Refugio 'Cuco' Sánchez Saldaña
"Anoche estuve llorando"©1954, 'Cuco' Sánchez

"El aguacero ©1955, Tomás Méndez, sung by Miguel Aceves Mejía

"Cucurrucucu paloma"©1954, Tomás Méndez, sung by Lola Beltrán

"Juan Charrasqueado"©1954, Víctor Cordero, sung by Jorge Negrete

"Tata Dios"©1956, Valeriano Trejo, sung by Miguel Aceves Mejía

"Sacred Life"©1994, Ian Astbury, Billy Duffy, "The Cult"

"Otro poema de los dones"©1964, Jorge Luis Borges

"Where Corn Don't Grow,"©1990, Roger Murrah, Mark Allen Springer, sung by Travis Tritt

"Away in a Manger," by John McFarland, James Murray, 1885, sung by Tammy Wynette

The Iliad, Homer, translation by William Cullen Bryant, 1870
The Odyssey, Homer, translation by William Cullen Bryant, 1871

"Walk this World with Me"©1994, Heather Nova

"The Call of the Wild"©1907, Robert Service

Photo Credits:

Cover. Perry Higman, Becky the dog, Iowa City, Iowa,1968. Photo, Bea Higman

Back cover. Sandra, Perry Higman, on a rainy day in Paris, 2006. Photo, Jesse Higman

Frontispiece. Larry Deaver, N. Idaho backcountry. 2011. Photo, Dave Waag, *Off-Piste Magazine,* offpistemag.com

Frontispiece. Deb Copenhaver on Snake, Penticton, B.C., 1949. Photo, Art Chamberlain

Frontispiece. Dick Alt, Chet Higman, Dwight Watson, Hermann Ulrichs, climbing reconnaissance in the North Cascades,1936. Photo Hermann Ulrichs

Scraper, *Copenhaver Construction.* 2011. Photo, Guy Copenhaver

Airplane and barn, *Greg's Crop Care* (Greg and Kevin Leyva), Wilbur, Washington. 2010. Photo by Todd Rodrigues

Beside their truck, Cheryl and Lester Simmons, 40 years on the road together. 2013. Photo, Sandra Higman

Jesse Higman on tour with *Lollapalooza,* 1994, photo by Danny Clinch, *Danny Clinch Photography,* New York. dannyclinch.com

John von Neumann exits the corkscrew at Laguna Seca in his Ferrari 625 TRC, November, 1957, photo credit, Michael T. Lynch Archive

Francisco "Pancho" Villa and Emiliano Zapata in President Carranza's office, November, 1914, photo credit, *Mutual Film Company*

P. Higman, Steve Jeffries, West Rib, Mt. McKinley, 1992. Photo, Matt Chase

Doc and me, North Idaho backcountry. 2004. Photo, Denny Burmeister

The Vietnam Veterans Memorial. 2005. Photo, Shelley Higman

Chet Higman, Pinnacle Peak, 1937. Photo, Bea Kauffman

Bardomiano Balbuena (in hat), wife, child, and father-in-law, Valle de Bravo, 1956. Photo, Bea Higman

Summit of Aneto, Spanish Pyrenees, Kate Schertenlieb, Denny Burmeister, Perry Higman, 2006. Photo, Denny Burmeister

Summit Mt. Rainier, Shelley Higman, Perry Higman, 1996, photo, Tom Couraud

Shelley Higman, Rome. 2005. Photo, Jesse Higman

The author shoeing near Cheney, Washington, 1980. Photo by Bea Higman

Deb Copenhaver being recognized by the crowd at National Finals Rodeo 2010. Photo, Molly Morrow, *Molly Morrow Photography*, Ellensburg, Washington. mollymorrow.com

Some of the poems in this collection are previously published:

"A Photograph of Zapata", *Remembrances of Wars Past,* Editor, Henry Tonn

"For Jesse", *Silver Boomers,* Edited by Greene, Haigler, Riley-Bishop, Rollins

"Love"   *Apple Valley Review*

'Vietnam Veterans Memorial"
                           Southern Maine Review

"Roy Rogers and Me"
                           New York Times Magazine

"Country Sunday"   *A Southern Journal*

"Unopened Gifts"   *Main Channel Voices*

"NASCAR"   *Fried Chicken and Coffee Journal*

Other books by Perry Higman:

Love Poems from Spain and Spanish America,
(translations), City Lights Booksellers, San Francisco

Sueñan, Lloran, Cantan, Poems for Children,
(translations), Eastern Washington University Press

Some of Higman's translations also appear in:

Gauchos, Takarajima Books

Memories of Daughters, Park Lane Press

Art and Love, Metropolitan Museum of Art